T0199176

God created The World in Seven Days

By: Melanie Guice

WestBow Press books may be ordered through booksellers or by contacting:

WestBow Press
A Division of Thomas Nelson & Zondervan
1663 Liberty Drive
Bloomington, IN 47403
www.westbowpress.com
844-714-3454

Because of the dynamic nature of the Internet, any web addresses or links contained in this book may have changed since publication and may no longer be valid. The views expressed in this work are solely those of the author and do not necessarily reflect the views of the publisher, and the publisher hereby disclaims any responsibility for them.

Any people depicted in stock imagery provided by Getty Images are models, and such images are being used for illustrative purposes only.
Certain stock imagery © Getty Images.

Interior Image Credit: Melanie Guice

ISBN: 978-1-6642-3087-3 (sc)
ISBN: 978-1-6642-7509-6 (hc)
ISBN: 978-1-6642-3088-0 (e)

Library of Congress Control Number: 2021907544

Print information available on the last page.

WestBow Press rev. date: 08/05/2022

WESTBOW
PRESS®
A DIVISION OF THOMAS NELSON
& ZONDERVAN

This book belongs to:

_____

_____

This book is dedicated to:

My Mommy and Daddy
My Sisters and Cousins
My Grandmas and Grandpas
My Aunties and Uncles
My God Parents
My Pastor
My Church Family

Illustrator Notes

I am Melanie Guice and I hope you enjoy my book. I wanted to show you how our God created the world in six days and rested on the seventh day. When I asked my Grandmother "How was the world created?" She explained it to me and then went out to buy me my own bible. I was so excited to learn how God created the world. (Children of Color Story Book Bible 2019) After reading it, I wanted to draw and write the story.

In the beginning

1st
Day

God created
light from the
darkness.

2nd
Day

God created
The sky.

3rd Day

God created the seas, plants, trees, fruit, and grain.

God
Separated -
Day and night

6th Day

God Created the animals.

God
rested,
After He finished

Resource Page

The Children's of Color Story Book Bible (2019)
The Story of Creation *by Children of Color*

Printed in the United States
by Baker & Taylor Publisher Services